Philosophy is…

Poetry

barZENder

WHY PHI?

Published by Cherrymoon Media

FOREWORD

Scarcity is a myth perpetuated by those who never learned to share...

CONTENTS

Barzender

There once was a curious bartender
Epic tales from her journey she'd render
She served them with joy
But her purpose, unemployed
So, with new mindset, evolved the barZENder

The life she had known was the past
In her heart, these memories would last
So she closed out her tab
Gave thanks all she'd had
Amazed years had gone by so fast

Not certain what else she might do
To set stage for a meaningful Act II
She picked up paper and pen
Found her garden of Zen
Here's the outcome, without further ado...

Cheers

There are many I wish that I could thank
In this, my first book
First, to my editor and mentors
For the hours of guidance it took

Equally crucial, to my tribe and crew
Who read all those countless drafts
And for every sage bringer of wisdom
Constantly guiding me on my path

Family and friends, who have loved me
Even when I deserved it least
And honorable mention to ill-fated loves
That sought to tame my inner beast

Above all the rest, my sincerest thanks
To them that thrashed me to the core
Because it's in the wake of choices we make
We grow stronger than before

These poems have become my Zen
Noble truths tempo'd through rhyme
So, cheers to those – past, present, and future
Who ignite and fuel my drive!

Bio-Mixology

Magic Potion #9

Ingredients:
*Double Shot - Growth Mindset
*Single Pour - Spiritual Philosophy
*Splash - Cultural Paradox
(My carefully measured recipe...)

Directions:
1. Shake 'til Chilled & Served Straight Up
2. Strain & Pour Into a Glass of "WTF?!?"
3. Dash of Manifestation to Float
4. Garnished w/Gratuity &
Served w/Love Notes:

A magical incantation

For you and yours to imbibe...

Thanks for sticking with me,

And taking me along for the ride!!!

Think

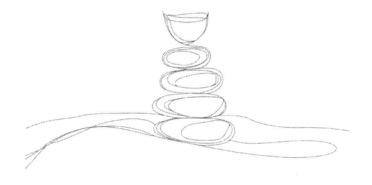

Consumption of knowledge is encouraged...
...Please think responsibly!

Opt

Some say, "That glass is half full"
Which is often misconstrued
Faith in good won't come from hope
Just an intentional attitude

Optimism is not a wish
That the world will bend your way
Instead, a promise to yourself
To be grateful for each day

In peering through life's glasses
They prove only what you think
Some spiked with victim mindset
Tempts us all to sip this toxic drink

We must own up to our actions
Seek forgiveness above all else
Asked of those we might have tread
But mostly, asked of ourselves

Life happens for you, there is no 'happens to'
All the woes you face in life, lead right back to you
Owning our own actions, the only path to peace
Finds gratitude and abundance, it's all in how we speak

When what the world may bring your way
Is no longer of your concern
Then you're living the philosophy
To give thanks for what you've learned

Wonder

We wonder why there's evil, and just how it came to be
We wonder why we can't connect, and are we even WE?!?

We wonder when the days may grant, to us, our final prize
Can we not be living gifted? To find peace
must we all die?

We wonder what may cease our path, and how we may desert
We wonder who will try to block, whomever might we hurt?

We wonder why it seems so tough, to get by getting by
We blame faux foes for our own woes, seeking first to
demonize

We wonder why we're grieving, asking "What does it all mean?
How did we let it get this way, and is there just no in
between?"

Above all else we wonder, if our lives will leave a mark
But if all believe themselves as 'good,' are we groping in the
dark?

The reason there is evil, in a world of so much good
Is that good and evil concepts are rarely understood

Nobody is born evil, we all receive a soul
It's the choices that we make with it, that determine our life's
toll

What some may see as evil, a malicious awful plan
Is often just a fearful soul, that needs a helping hand

We're all both good and evil, two souls linked as one
There is no goodness measure, a life's goodness is its sum

Power might not come from above (unless you count the sun)
Power won't creep from below (unless mantles comes undone)

The only power that can enact, the purpose of self-hood
Is the power that's found within to best serve the common
good

Blink

Philosophers don't seek the 'what'
Which merely asks the link
We seek the 'why' within the ask
Wishing not to settle at the brink

In living life, we share the cues
To ponder mysteries we shrink
When by sharing in the knowing
We may find some greater sync

Like the proverbial horse to water
You can't make people think
But by teaching them to logic
They come to know their own instincts

So, just maybe, by writing these thoughts
(Using paper, pen, and ink)
I may in fact open other's eyes
To change their own life in a blink?

Goddess

For centuries subjected
To patriarchal rule

Warfare gods, cheered on high
Warrior goddess, played the fool

They've told the fairer sex we're weak
More daughters than can count

They've told their heirs:
"Take what you want, this world is yours to mount!"

But the feminine is far from weak
(As every mother knows)

We can handle the horrors of birthing life
(Some fathers can't handle the show)

So why is it some say to girls
"A man must be the king?"

Because deep down even misogynists know:
The Power of P@&$% rules all things!

Seeds

Truth is much like a tree
And with every seed that's sown
We learn the loudest mass beliefs
Do not define the known

Truth lies in our own virtue
To be found inside our soul
But what to do when memories seem
To never cease their anxious hold?

We rarely share honestly
Emotional stings and aching pains
Instead, we state upon repeat
The same pleasing refrains

So, what if these painful feelings
Were the least essential facts?
Maybe vulnerable moral support
Teach us all to more graciously act?

Hybrid your seeds with others'
Ethically root your sprouting mind
As the only way any tree grows strong
Is to stand the test of time

Mani/Medi

Meditation is essential for clarity
But misunderstanding breeds inner discourse
It's falsely assumed we must sit perfectly still
Lasered focus, cleared mind, hummed chords

This misinterpretation, I'd like to fix
And through my own tale, share a bit of fact
A blank mind isn't the only trick
It's tending of soul through simple acts

As many may struggle to spot their good nature
Good fortune, and inner spark that shines bright
To impart the gift of better knowing yourself
Here's a list of ways to spot your own light:

> Read, journal, poetry, pets, music, art, nature walks,
> gratitude, gardening, hobbies, cooking, self-prayer &
> self-care...

All good habits for redressing
Those emotional wounds and burns
So, gift yourself a few moments of peace
By just sitting to watch the world turn!

Pagan

Lingering puritan norms
Fed to the world's angry trolls
Those that seek to become the Judge
Though it's often been said, not their role?

To separate the church from the state
Wouldn't that be a sight?
Dibs given first to rights of those
Who directly funded said rights?

Some clutching tight 'divine' prophets
While perverting their holy scripts
If a fabric we're meant to be weaving
Why do so many seek only to rip?

Just for now, let's speak some truths
And bid our judgment be restrained
As prophets were once just philosophers too
So, won't their purposes remain?

From our own sincere convictions
As to whom we think is right
Maybe it's just in stepping back
Clear vision comes into sight?

During this thoughtful journey
Please suspend prior (dis)belief
To bridge a bit of knowledge gapped
Grant your logic a sense of relief!

Ancestral artifacts reveal
That our pondering once sought
A belief in something greater
For mere beasts, we were not

Anthropological markers shown
Before modern zealotry's reign
Knowledge shared led to innovation
Curiosity valued, apathy disdained

Questioning of the unknown
Man's most abundant rite
Has led somehow to wicked acts
In seeking sole claim on might

From talismans to carved walls
Created first in the human mind
The ultimate creation story
Evolved a species in real time

Storytelling has been our nature
From constellations to the tides
We yearned to learn our place in things
In this unknown cosmic ride

We now ponder, "Why is Stonehenge?
How do sphynx and pyramids incept?
Who first praised this unknown source
And where lie our greatest missteps?"

Art predated ritual
Or could that have been reversed?
There's just no way to know for sure
As wisdom exponentially dispersed

Ancient shrines and altars stand
Monuments to the first
By many names, but known as light
Throughout history, a worship rehearsed

Later, an age of epic myths
Similarly writ to endure
To give our growing mind ethos
And for its ego, to reassure

Mythology, a stepping stone
From celestial to strife
As gods were given vanity
To mirror man's own life

God and goddess cast as scornful
Petty, jealous, and enraged
Bowing to their feral wants
Consistently misbehaved

In trying to sort good from evil
Man authored a lasting tale
About the curious girl who opened a box
Hope stayed, so evil prevailed

Then came this common era
When the many became the one
Pagans killed like outlaws
Disbelievers hid and shunned

An image emerged slowly
From an often uttered tome
Unlikely fables told on repeat
Like a virgin birthing a son

(I hesitate to include this
But for the sake of quote-worthy rhymes
Just for once, could we all ask,
"Why so obsessed with women's hymens?!?")

The theology of a savior shared
By religions throughout time
Languages speak the same allegory
People dying for who may be right

Governed by masculine energy
What unsurprisingly lied in store?
We continually murdered our own species
Proof only our god was worth the war

Generations do forget
While still sharing this decree
It's said that in the very beginning
There was but man, a garden, and tree

He first was granted reason
To peer up and look around
At every type of bountiful bush
Growing up from the under the ground

His human nature stirred on earth
And so, was ribbed a mate
To bask in all that's well and good
Within this heavenly place

From there, this tale veers off course
As you may soon recognize
The claim that knowledge breeds discourse
Hidden (yet again) in front of your eyes

So how is it that knowing, is perceived to be a sin?
And why must a woman's source, rely solely on him?
Could it be that weaker men, have known this all along?
As Pagans hailed: Sacred Feminine, is infinitely stronger!

So let's all give this moment's thought
Within reason, to form greater beliefs
Maybe connection of the human spirit,
Is that same curious nature perceived?

Our existence has been spiritual
From first our fire sparked
Now known to be mere chemistry
Electric charge from brain to heart

But the heart's vibrational magnet
Can't explain this crucial ask:
What initial spark sets fire to souls
To Illuminate their path?

Merely science, sad but true
But let's take the next logical step
Could it be that when we feel as one
Spiritual science somehow connects?

The earliest believers
Long before the first harvest sown
Praised nature and their source of light
As these were all things known...

Feel

Feel it.

Learn it.

Grow From It.

Be kind,

Always:

To others, whenever possible.

To Yourself, a non-negotiable.

Rinse.

Repeat.

Frequency

Manifest is just a verb
To think with energy
Creating acts within a thought
Thoughts have a frequency

Manifest means making ripples
With every stone we cast
Karma in its purest form
As future follows past

Manifest means sowing
And knowing time will reap
Manifest is a language
That most already speak

Ignorance to manifest
Won't cease it in our acts
Like gravity, invisible
But in knowing, proves a fact

Manifestation is a super-power
With human minds, we possess
We all must first affect a cause
To cause an effect

Spark

In a child we must invest
To seek a play that makes them blessed
Not assuming our own opinion best
As this thought only minds the rest

Tell them that their work is art
A voice that whispers from the heart
Kindle in them a creative spark
To reinforce their effort's arc

Encourage them to always roam
You'll light a path to lead them home
Teach them that their joy's your own
And think as though your thoughts are known

A child's mind is like a scroll
Wide eyes are windows to their soul
Keen ears pick up more than the goal
Ideas we'd hoped not to extol

All we can do, in setting their course
Give them a map, point their compass due north
By magnetizing to them their means
Brought to them passion, to live beyond dreams

Soultending

Blinders on, some walk through life
Hiding from their wounds
Thinking what is best for us
Based on their sense of doom

That's why healing is essential
To see the clearest signs
Learn what you can from others
But it's your own soul's value to assign

Let's not assume our thoughts as 'best'
Life isn't superlative
'Most Likely to Succeed' does not
Factor into the world we live

Let us think ourselves instead
As gardeners constantly
In tending our own soul's soil first
Our acts prove what we believe

34

Grace

Give to yourself, a wealth of grace
To make more than a few mistakes

Grant for your life, the ample time
To let it all somehow align

Allow the chance, to self-reflect
Lessons you hope not to forget

Permit yourself, to ask repent
For every choice that came and went

Show thanks for all, tough lessons learned
And for every scar that you have earned

Cast your gaze upon, those lofty goals
That seek contentment in your soul

Envision yourself, on a nobler course
Hoping for the best, but prepared for worst

Look to the trials, to provide you tests
Fulfilling your purpose above all the rest

So, when you feel that deep heartache
And life, it seems to blow up in your face

Give to yourself, a wealth of grace
The universe, Darling, makes no mistakes!

Flow

Rage against the dying light
(Another poet said)
Taking notice of the darkness
As it creeps into your head

But, in my humble opinion
Can't say this, for me, rings true
As philosophers & poets alike
Seek to guide us to the proof

We rage because we're animals
Weaponizing words to engage
Legitimizing corrupt acts
As truth falls well beyond our gaze

There may be times to safely rage
To keep a life force finely tuned
For what we see as fading lights
May just be our own deep wounds

We think we rage to stay alive
We believe that we are right
We notice no clear indication,
That we rationalize this plight

Sometimes we must stand and fight
To guard our safety, and our own
But lashing out for feelings
This rage best stay unknown

Do not rage when lights get dim
It's just your fear of the unknown
Don't curse aloud your downward luck
(Unless you stub your toe!)

Apologize to all trespassed
To forgive yourself and grow
Now take a deep breath, count to ten
And go with (for once) the flow!

Tsk Tsk...

Let's play a little game
To provide a logical reframe
Casting of stones, not my aim
Your power, instead, to forever reclaim

Can you feel your spirit strain?
Do you think your mind too tame?
Sense the dimming of an inner flame?
Flickering out under the thoughts of fame?
How do you speak to your own name?
Do you seek others' approving acclaim?
Are your inner demons sounding insane?
Do your words seem to inadvertently maim?
Spoken unto you and to others the same?
Are you inclined to seek 1st only to blame?
Does confidence seem to flee as fast as it came?
If yes to all, welcome to the monster of shame!

Many think that spotting faults will lead to our sense of 'lame'
But it's when we deny human nature
The spark of self-doubt becomes inflamed

The trick to sidestepping this soul-crushing self-disdain:
Is by calling out our <u>humanness</u>,
Shame's given a humane name

Human

Feelings aren't flaws
Just evolved mammals' gifts
Our survival super-power
From which higher minds can sift

That which threatens
Them that calm
Those who create
A shared sense of awe...

Species' interconnection
In all its many forms,
Requires vulnerability
To better seek social norms

So, when society tells us,
"Don't let 'em see you cry"
You may be denying the very thing
That makes you human in others' eyes

Act

*The shouting of man-made law is deafening
And provides only questions*

*The whisper of natural law is harmonious
And provides only answers*

Showstopper

If you are told by anyone, your joy won't be found in song
Stand square up, clear your throat
And belt it out that they are wrong!

If, for whatever reason, you're told never to dance
Prove your body's lust for life
And express movement at every chance!

Who would think to tell a child, "Never, ever sing?"
Because they can't, so you can't too?
Words to share in self-limiting

Who would ever tell a child, "Minimize your heart's glee?"
I can only guess a saddened soul
Who's never felt that free

Instead, make your own rules, and live at your own pace
As you are the only person,
Daily looking at your own face

Dance your steps, write your lyrics, hum your heart's tune
Time to let the world know
You're here taking up room!

Sync with life's most curious beats, and take those scary steps
Be your soul's own showstopper
And find out what exactly you possess!

10ƒ

As

Many will say:

If at first you don't

Succeed? Well try, try again!

Words offered up to fallen souls

Advice we'll here and now reattend

Successful lives are never measured

In counting the number of tries they ace

Anecdotally, it's in those epic failures

That we may build our sturdiest base

By learning from each try's failing

What we seek to find, we earn

Even our most epic fails

Teach us to spot

Our errs with

Discern

When a fallen soul can rally

To stand and face a fall...

They've shown the world

Their bravest of acts:

To walk, we all first crawl!

Wager

Life is but a bet we take
A die that we must cast
Ante'd on the wishful yen
New moments will surpass

But if the gamble doesn't pay
Then whatever shall we do?
Maybe we shouldn't try at all,
Wouldn't that be just fine, too?

But life is not a stack of chips
Of which, there's many more
Living is not a roulette wheel
And there's no dealer keeping score

So, hedge your one and only bet
To seek a future you won't regret
Lead others to wager on themselves, too
Simply by going all in on you!

Light a match, burn the boats
And give yourself zero outs
Someday soon you'll find meaning
When your heart's 'tell' leaves no doubts

Paradox

Sayings heard aren't what they seem
As if echoed in some lucid dream
Little quips shared, confound us no end
Lost in translation, the meaning may bend

That which doesn't kill us, makes us strong?
Those we love hurt us, to keep us from harm?
Lightning (they say), can only strike once?
So how do great artists hone any nuance?

A mind that's inspired, is one of a fool?
And genius follows, the madness rule?
Keep your friends close, and your enemies too?
Well then who should we be listening to?

It's no wonder it takes us so long to learn
Such simple wisdom has its own place and turn

So, this advice I must give, may seem paradox:

To live the life you've always dreamed...
Get the F@#$ outside the box!

Choreo

Each step we take, a step we've gone
No matter forwards or backwards, our footprints linger on

Leaving treads on others, and stomps on ourselves
Twirling about to inspire, our own soul's greater wealth

Life's surest paths are not cleared, by any step-by-step hack
We get only brief cues, for dotted lines to be dashed

Courage earned in stumbling, if yet once again, we can stand
And learn the steps to the rhythm, of our spirit's soulful band

If you feel your 2 left feet, are not quite up to the task
Just close your eyes, take a breath, and for a sign, merely ask

Still your mind, feel the rhythm, follow your heart's true pace
To choreograph a dance of future wins, it's all in how we race

Utility

Utility best?
As many may say
Subjective moral relativism
That seems guided in ethical ways

Riding the high seas much fabled
Hedon pirates' shanty'd remorse
First mapped the deepest of waters
Seeking horizon to steady their course

When coastal waters start churning
And stormy tides get a bit rough
It's hard to see the waves breaking
In the distance near treacherous bluffs

When lost sailors near port, on the darkest of nights
Seek welcoming shores, search their eyes for a light
With but skyline to lead, how to reach safe harbor home?
Not be dragged out by currents, left sailing seaward to roam?

In a flash, a lighthouse sends sign
That this squalled excursion shan't be maligned
But as quickly as it shone, this guiding light is rapidly gone
A crew left to wander in wonder, and to bravely steady on

Then a second flash illuminates the dune
And so sails are set towards avoiding ruin
As wind billows the main along this new route
The signal once again stops, the light source spins out

With no way else to find the land
The lighthouse serves its only plan
To spin around and confuse sight
For all the travelers lost in the night

A sailor knows to count the flash
Pacing tempo, distance, and space
But without a lifetime of high tides learned
There's little way to know our boat's place

The means by which we guide our ships
Can't cater only to the shore
So, look onward to your own north star
And be lost at sea no more!

Trust in the countless leagues you've sailed
For every knot, and each rudder adjust
Once you learn to harness life's tidal waves
Your soul will never rust

Let the bravest of seas fill your veins,
(And Jimmy's pirate tradition forever remain)
As the wind fills your sails, may your voyage so gain
The ethical pull to best guide your soul's sole aim!

Meta

Ethics are life's guidelines
By which we all must choose
To live by rules we'd like to see
The entire world would use

Ethics aren't indictments
Or moral judgement calls
They merely offer guidance:
"Take no claim in others' fall"

Ethical behavior
Serves well beyond our scope
As there is no intrinsic good
In stealing others' hope

The Golden Rule recited
For most, our ethics taught
Imparts to us compassion
And teaches us to 'ought'

But the moral, lost in use
As kids most often learn
"All that's good = what's good for me"
And so, ignore another's turn

Being good based on yourself
(This rule we speak to youth)
Does not address the greater good
Our fundamental truth

The base of ethics clearly states
A Deontological fact:
We have no right to know a thing
But impede another's tack

Dishonesty, in all its forms
Protecting fragile ego
Free to simply choose a choice
We can't for others veto

The duty of our reasoning
(Realized through foresight)
Assumes contracted virtue
As empathy shines a light

Integrity, a noble gig
To which, we ought apply
For to live a life of virtue
And trust in another, we rely

This abundant gift of free will
Ours to model for the good
So how could we impart this truth
To be less misunderstood?

Teach kids that others differ
Their thoughts aren't for the rest
Let's impart to future thinkers
Honesty is the basic test

Grow

Human Paradox:

Beastly Body, Divine Mind,

Yin & Yang of Soul!

Purpose

A cure for all that ails, my dear
A saltwater dose of sweat, sea, or tears

A healing for all that cuts, my friend
Will give you the strength to face it once again

A poison in all the potions, my pretty
Grants super-human desire to topple a city

A shift in all the labor, my team
Imagine the same person you'd wish to be seen

A mother of all doubts, my fam
Reminds us these thoughts rarely serve us in the end

A goal of all growth, my love
For each other always, to go beyond and above

A kink of all taboo, my pet
Give them a thrill they won't soon forget

A base for all virtue, my muse
First own your acts, let others own their own, too

A claim of all ethics, my ilk
Learning to weave our shabby threads into sparkling silk

A notion of all Zen, my scribes
Simply take a deep breath, and see where this rides

A meaning for all purpose, my light
Feed the spark from within, and let it ignite

A secret to manifesting, my tribe
First feeling thoughts, and soon time will abide...

Co-Inspiring

Often in phrases we use, we divide the end from the means
These terms, at times, broad terminal slights, distracting us
from our routines
Counterintuitive oxymorons, the language of a fool?
Turned around and tossed on the ground, by those who find it
obscene

One such phrase, to be revealed, is an undervalued gift
Based on humanity's single shared goal: Helping each other
over the rifts
Philosophers and prophets: teachers and counselors all
Have been lighting the way and keeping at bay our soul's
catastrophic shifts

My list of questionable phrases is long
But lucky for you, there's only 1 verse to this song
'Cause in my darkest of nights, wise speakers shined their
light
And saved me from my own sense of wronged

These soothsayers, they guided me, and I've forever shifted
my course
Taught me to limit my limiting beliefs – the self-trust to put
cart before horse
This is why the phrase 'Self-Help' could never begin to impart
The offering of hands and a brand new life plan, striking gold
within the source

So maybe we could choose, a more valid word co-op?
For my vote, "Co-Inspiring" may be the right swap!
They who are inspired, are inspiring, paying forward
humanity's dues
Help is to show each other to grow, so first, the Self must be
taught

Diva

Your memories are your stage
Your mistakes are your set
Your bio is your prop costume
Your triumphs are your spotlight

Your mindset tuned to the desired key
Your feelings are the varied beats
Your words, the only notes you need
Your acts are your opus arrangement

Your intentions are your director
Your story whispers your cues
Your impact is your ability to connect
Your legacy is in your reviews

Your past is your hero's journey
Your struggle is your character's arc
Your present is your vision quest
Your future is your mic drop

Your future is your mic drop
Your future is your mic drop

Shhh

How-To: Find YOUR Own Voice

1) STOP TALKING!!!
2) close eyes & shut out noise
3) focus on mind & body poise
4) slow deep breaths & savor the air
5) find that which brings joy & become aware
6) gift of thanks & receive a full cup...

Harness the mind body rhythm
&
YOUR soul will speak up!

Bewilder

The human mind seeks wisdom
Parables to guide our way
To learn from logical pitfalls
We travel back to an ancient place
Among the eldest monuments
Built by and for the human race
Amid the philosophic ruins
Stands the doorway to a Cave
The Cave doesn't claim what's true
Just imparts means to behave
The Cave does not teach right from wrong
It's shared only to tempo our pace
It speaks to all life's journeys
That baser instincts may be our grave
Tempting us to venture out
Seeking knowledge, always brave

In this cave, live prisoners
In shackles, illogical slaves
Unawakened to the world outside
These lives we'd seek to save
Thought prisoners bound to sit and stare
Their heads locked front to face
Toward moving shadows on a wall
A source, they cannot trace
The shadows on the wall are blank
With no details, simply shapes
A back-lit human puppet show
Cast by the suns own warming rays
But this fool's den offers up no warmth
Just a hole and human stave
With but shadows on the wall to guide
Any wonder we can't behave?

Seeking wisdom from the cave wall
Would be a shared mistake
As all cave-dwelling people know
There's just no way to escape
Until we make that first move
To turn our heads and face
The bright light shining from behind
Eyes fixed, for once, on grace
Tilt your head and break the chains
Keep all your doubts at bay
To join the other escapees
Stepping out beyond the nave
Blinking eyes in wonder
Adjust to their first day
Strange to those unwilling to leave
Resigning themselves to stay

Stories brought down from above
As wanderers return to pave
A freedom path to wisdom
For the ignorance enslaved
The trek to knowing anything
This ascent from whence we rave
Enlightened and unenlightened both
All share in this dismay
Life is often tough to figure
Treading water on current waves
As walking in and out of light
Could bewilder any knave
Turn your head and cast your eyes
Let chains of 'knowing' fall away
From the ancient gifts of Plato
Behold, The Allegory of the Cave!

Evolve

Our nature pushes us to grow
An earthly evolution flow

The inner push and outer tug
Ideas that spread with nod and shrug

But this eternal force must stay
And keep the species on its way

To carry out the greatest feats
We soon must grow from our defeats

The change we seek may feel like flaws
But this ignores evolving laws

In the end, flaws make us strong
Embrace them first, and grow along...

Magic

I do not believe in life hacks
But this is what I've known
Put your dreams in writing
And share them with your own
In messages to tribe and peers
Shared journeys' future woes
When just speaking future triumphs
Could pave more well-lit roads
For those that want a life trick
To see the magic form
Try writing from your future self
And your goals become your norm...

~~~

A Note From The Author

To Those Curious Readers Who Have Come This Far:

This poem was my first, created on a whim of inspiration after a text to a dear muse. (If you don't have a 'manifestation buddy,' find/create one!!!) Within weeks, this collection of poems seemed to fall out of my head and into verse. As if by magic...

Sometimes, you must lean into the unknown to create what you didn't even know you desired. To truly find your purpose, try letting go of the need to control fate, while opening your mind to new means of finding meaning. Your journey may pleasantly surprise you.

Seek creativity, give yourself permission to explore. Be willing to be 'beyond bad' at that thing that sparks your soul. This is the first and single most important step towards becoming great!

Cheers,
bZ

Background

Serving Self 1st =
Surviving

Serving Others 1st =
Thriving

Origins

Crafting a worthwhile dream?

                                        ... *36 years*

Trial & error, practice & failure?

                                        ... *5 years*

Believing yourself as intrinsically flawed?

                                ... A lifetime trained

The feeling of missing out on life?

                                ... A life force detained

        ***** Karmic Gut Punch**

                        ... A split second remains ***

Pain seeks to cope, creativity begins to flow?

                                        ... 6 months

Removal of limiting beliefs in order to grow?

                                ... 3 months (But TBC'd)

Write the book you've always dreamed?

                                        ... 6 weeks

Believing yourself to be worthy?

                                        ... Daily

The feeling of fulfilling your unique purpose?

                                        ... Abundance!!!

The moment in the middle,
When the stars align
Ripples set in motion,
To erode that which resigns
Boulders and stones once stacked by me,
Now, to redefine
To let go of the past,
And finally live by my design
While it evolved ever-more quickly,
And picks up pace even still
When I lay out my soul's evolution
The power of manifestation is re-instilled!

Sometimes the Karmic gut punch, is not showing you the end
Simply an echo, brought back from the silenced voice within...

If only I could go back in time, to any painful marker from before?
To tell my past self-loathing mind, what exactly lay in store
But would that defeat the purpose, as all invaders of my peace
Left the cuts and scars, that now proudly mark my inner beast!!!

Tricky

Just a tricky little bio
If curiosity's been peaked
Let's give but brief introduction
Look at the thinker of these thoughts we read
Each line stands as a symbol
Really, not much to impart
You've already read the vulnerable truth
Nestled within her heart

Right now, you may be wondering
You may think this bio daft
And reckon that this entire pursuit
Needs some precious time granted back

Much to say, though not enough space on the page
As to bore is never my aim
Just a couple more brief stanzas to cite
Of whom this book is claimed
Readers, you've made it, can't thank you enough!

(Now, to answer this riddle, you must 1st look up....)

Made in the USA
Columbia, SC
17 November 2024

46207838R00054